Riding the Ox Home

Riding the Ox Home

STAGES ON THE PATH OF ENLIGHTENMENT

JOHN DAIDO LOORI

Edited by Konrad Ryushin Marchaj

SHAMBHALA · BOSTON & LONDON · 2002

SHAMBHALA PUBLICATIONS, INC.
Horticultural Hall
300 Massachusetts Avenue
Boston, Massachusetts 02115
www.shambhala.com

Originally published as *Path of Enlightenment: Stages in a
Spiritual Journey* by Dharma Communications.

9 8 7 6 5 4 3 2 1

First Shambhala Edition
Printed in the United States of America

♾ This edition is printed on acid-free paper that meets the
American National Standards Institute z39.48 Standard.
Distributed in the United States by Random House, Inc.
and in Canada by Random House of Canada Ltd

LIBRARY OF CONGRESS CATALOGING-IN-PUBLICATION DATA
Loori, John Daido.
Riding the ox home: stages on the path of enlightenment/John Daido
Loori; edited by Konrad Ryushin Marchaj.
p.   cm.
ISBN 1-57062-951-X
1. Enlightenment (Zen Buddhism)   I. Title: Stages on the path of
enlightenment.   II. Marchaj, Konrad Ryushin.   III. Title.
BQ9288 .L664   2002
294.3'442—dc21   2002017664

Contents

Editor's Note

THE TEN OX-HERDING PICTURES ARE REPRODUCTIONS OF ink paintings by Gyokusei Jikihara Sensei, a Japanese master of calligraphy and a teacher in the Obaku School of Zen. They were painted by Jikihara Sensei in 1982, during one of his many visits to Zen Mountain Monastery, and presented to the Monastery as a gift. They are a beautiful example of traditional Chinese-style *nanga* brush painting. The originals are on display at Zen Mountain Monastery.

The corresponding poems describing one's progress on a spiritual journey were composed by Zen Master Kuoan in the twelfth century. They were translated by Kazuaki Tanahashi and John Daido Loori, and further modified by Daido Loori in an attempt to create images and metaphors more closely linked to the mountains and rivers surrounding Zen Mountain Monastery.

KONRAD RYUSHIN MARCHAJ
Editor

Introduction

THE PATH OF ENLIGHTENMENT IS A SPIRITUAL JOURNEY OF discovering our true nature. But the fact is that from the very beginning there is nothing to acquire. From the beginning, we are perfect and complete, lacking nothing. During a spiritual journey, in taking up and engaging specific practices, we come to personally experience and verify the reality of that perfection.

Shakyamuni, the historical Buddha, attained enlightenment through a thoroughgoing study of his life in a seated meditation called *zazen.* At the moment of his realization, he directly experienced the very foundation of reality. He exclaimed, "I, all beings, and the great earth have at once entered the Way." With that statement, the Buddha was unequivocally pointing to his and our intrinsic perfection. A genuine spiritual journey directs itself to this matter. The journey is a return to our original perfect state, the ground of being available to us at every moment. In Zen, we call that perfect state the True Self, the most fundamental aspect of our life. Each one of us is born with it and will die with it. Some will realize the fact of that perfection, some will not. Nonetheless, it is always present.

Since there is nothing external to attain—nothing that anyone can give us and nothing that we can receive—the spiritual journey is a ceaseless process of investigating ourselves, of digging through the layers of our conditioning to reach the ground of our being. Conditioning is unavoidable. It begins at birth and continues throughout our lives, perpetuated by our culture, parents, teachers, religions, peers, and society. We all define ourselves through it. When we reach adulthood we find ourselves living our lives out of this deeply ingrained script. At some point, we may sense that something is not quite right. Feeling unreal, meaningless, or perpetually dissatisfied despite plenty of material goods and good experiences, we become aware of an undercurrent of suffering that permeates our lives. Questions begin to arise, and with them the impetus to find our true humanity and to become completely free.

Each step of a spiritual journey involves this crucial turning point of becoming aware of our most profound questions. In acknowledging our impulse for clarity, it is then possible to develop our aspiration for enlightenment. Once we are conscious of our deepest yearnings we can begin our practice, realize ourselves, and share that wisdom with others. At each stage along the way this cycle of practice, realization, and actualization is repeated. Again and again and again.

Each step requires the questions of great doubt—"Who am I? What is truth? What is reality? What is life? What is death?" These questions change as the spiritual journey unfolds, but there are always questions. They are the cutting edge of practice. We also need to have faith. Unless we trust ourselves and the process, there is no possibility of being fully engaged. If there is no trust, skepticism and cynicism arise and we don't receive what the practice offers. Along with great doubt and great faith we need great determination, the ability to persevere in spite of all odds. Thirteenth-century Japanese Zen Master Eihei Dogen said, "To study the Way is to study the self, to study the self is to forget the self, to forget the self is to be enlightened by the ten thousand things." Studying the self is the most difficult undertaking any of us will ever engage in our lives. The spiritual journey requires incredible effort because the self is specifically conditioned not to be forgotten. In the process of exploring the self, resistances will come up. But when great doubt, great faith, and great determination function together in balance, we keep the spiritual journey alive.

Each step of the way is filled with pearls—accomplishments and insights, and fraught with perils—corresponding complications and dangers. The pearls are the discoveries within ourselves that nourish and empower us, and allow us to help others. They shine right at the outset of our journey and continue throughout because this journey is a process of coming face-to-face with our original perfection. The perils are the sticking places, nests, distractions, and detours. The spiritual evolution itself creates new tests all along the way. We start with our collection of problems and we create new ones as the process of clarification develops.

When we are presented with a map of a terrain, we don't confuse the picture for the reality of the landscape we are walking through. We need to keep this distinction in mind when reading a description of a spiritual journey. A description of a path is not the path itself. No two people experience the same spiritual journey, so we can only speak in general terms about spiritual maturation. A true spiritual journey is beyond time and space, history and culture, guidelines and descriptions. Within every religion and spiritual tradition there are accounts of a genuine spiritual search. The stages and the characteristics of the stages are remarkably similar. Because of this universality it is helpful to create maps that point out the landmarks we may encounter, in this case using the language that arises from Zen practice.

In the traditional Zen monasteries of Asia, spiritual training was not explicitly delineated. To a beginning student it seemed to be a mysterious and organic process. Although the teacher knew what was going on, that is, where a student was in terms of their understanding and what they still needed to realize and clarify, the student wasn't necessarily aware of this. With the arrival of Japanese teachers in the West, this approach continued. I went through my entire training without any gauge of where I was, what I needed to do, or where the gaps were, other than from what came up in private interviews with my teacher. Usually, there was very little, if any, dialogue during these encounters, because they primarily involved working directly with *koans*, apparently paradoxical stories specifically designed to short-circuit the linear and descriptive states of mind. The teacher would either indicate that I should go on to the next koan or urge me to penetrate deeper the one I was working on. I had very little sense of what was going on. This tradition of teaching a student without providing a reference point is deeply ingrained in the East, but it is not so easily embraced in the West, where we are obsessed with wanting to know how we are doing and with having some way of measuring our progress and comparing ourselves with others.

In ancient Japan, if a person wanted to study the martial arts, they would go to a master and ask to become a student. If the master accepted them, they began their training. The training would continue for any number of years until, at some point, the master would say that the student was ready to start teaching on their own. When a student began training they would receive a white belt to hold their uniform together. As they practiced for many, many years, that white belt would get very dirty, because it is the one part of the uniform that traditionally was never washed. After six or seven years of putting the gear on and taking it off every day, the white belt became so stained that it could only be called a black belt. A student became "the black belt" along with their uniform. It was a gradual, almost indiscernible process. The wide range of colored belts we now associate with progress in the martial arts was introduced only recently, primarily for Westerners who seemed to need a well-defined sense of their place in the hierarchy. So now there are yellow belts and green belts and brown belts and blue belts, in addition to the white belt of the beginner and the black belt of the accomplished practitioner.

A similar situation was encountered in Zen. In my days of Zen study, I and all the other students really wanted to have a sense of what we had accomplished and of the challenges to come. For these reasons we have created at Zen Mountain Monastery a somewhat arbitrary but helpful map of training, based on a series of paintings from Chinese antiquity known as "The Ox-Herding Pictures." They illustrate the spiritual development of a student, from the moment they begin their spiritual quest until the completion of their training, when they become a teacher in their own right.

There are several different collections of the ox-herding pictures: a set of eight, a set of twelve, and a set of ten. The set of ten, compiled by Master Kuoan, is the most commonly used. At Zen Mountain Monastery, we adopted Kuoan's pictures and verses, roughly correlating them to ten stages of training. Of course, the process could be broken up into any number of steps. In experiencing the path there is no sense of distinct and fixed transitions. However, applying the ten ox-herding pictures to the dynamics of training, superimposing them on our experiences, allows us to talk about the spiritual journey and gives us a perspective on how the whole process works.

It seems to me that people train better when they are informed about and clear on what they are doing, especially when the maps are balanced with mysteries. Mystery is the heart of a true religious life. We continue to reserve plenty of space in Zen training for the great mysteries, and that balance is persistently at work in the teacher-student relationship. Although students may have a sense of where they are in terms of the stages of training, they really don't have a sense of where they are in terms of approval from the teacher regarding their understanding of the teachings and appreciation of nature of reality. Here, the empowerment has to come from within.

The spiritual journey is an incredible undertaking, an endless adventure of boundless opening. The ten Ox-Herding Pictures and the accompanying poems are a series of signposts. For some people they are helpful. For others they can become a hindrance. Please don't let them be a hindrance to you. Use them to clarify your path. Then, let them go.

Searching for the Ox

Vigorously cutting a path through the brambles,
  you search for the ox;

Wide rivers, eternal mountains, the path seems
  endless.

With strength depleted, and mind exhausted, you
  cannot find it.

There is only the gentle rustle of maple leaves,
  and the cicadas' evening song.

THE FIRST STAGE OF A SPIRITUAL JOURNEY HAS TO DO WITH becoming aware of the possibility that a spiritual search can be a directive force in our lives. It is the time when we focus on the doubts plaguing us and clarify the intent of our lives. What is it that we must accomplish during this lifetime? What is most important to us?

There are all kinds of searches. Sometimes the search is for psychological well-being, sometimes for physical well-being, and sometimes for spiritual well-being. Many people come in contact with spiritual traditions seeking something that is not necessarily within the province of what those traditions are able to address. Physical and psychological contentment are often by-products of spiritual training, but if we are primarily interested in becoming healthier or better adjusted, there are more appropriate ways of taking care of that. If we are concerned with realizing the ground of being, with understanding who and what we really are, then we have begun a spiritual journey. In Zen, the training is specifically designed to deal with these fundamental spiritual inquiries.

The search can't start until the question arises. If the aspiration for enlightenment has not manifested; if the doubts we are confronting are not a matter of life and death; if, indeed, there is no question; then obviously there is no answer. The question needs to come up if genuine practice is to begin.

Zen literature is full of stories that point to the importance of getting in touch with our beginner's mind, of cultivating the attitude of a student. Master Deshan was a great scholar of the Diamond Sutra, one of the key scriptures of Buddhism. He lived in China in the eighth century, during the T'ang Dynasty, the golden age of Zen. He was very well versed in the Diamond Sutra and known all over northern China as one of its outstanding commentators. He had heard that Zen was being promoted in southern China as a "special transmission outside the scriptures," and was enraged by the idea that one didn't need to know how to read or be acquainted with the sacred texts to be able to realize oneself. He traveled south to denounce this heresy.

This was a man who had no questions—he had all the answers. He was filled with the Diamond Sutra and concluded that he understood the teachings forwards and backwards. There wasn't a part of the sutra he couldn't quote perfectly and elaborate on brilliantly. When he arrived in the southern region he had an encounter with an old woman selling tea by the roadside who, by chance, happened to be a Zen adept. She questioned him: "In the Diamond Sutra it says, 'past mind cannot be grasped, future mind cannot be grasped, present mind cannot be grasped.' With which mind will you accept this tea if I offer it to you?" Deshan, dumbfounded, fell silent, having been thrown into a state of great doubt. Everything he thought he knew was of no help to him. In that instant, the solidity of his knowledge and acumen crumbled, and in its place opened a gaping dark void. The search began for him at that point. Before, there were no questions and no quest. He was dead in his expertise.

The old woman teacher revived him, and directed him to a monastery where he could continue to deepen his questioning and practice. He went off to study with Master Longtan, who took his inquiries and brought them into intense focus until, finally, Deshan broke through his doubts.

We begin our spiritual quest by bringing our doubts into view. Our questions need to be real, like the pain we feel living an inauthentic life. And they need to be clear. In general, we don't really look deeply at what we are doing, and why. We don't investigate ourselves and the premises of our lives. We hesitate to articulate what is most important to us. Entering a spiritual path, we raise our consciousness and clarify our purpose.

Once this happens, the groundwork is set for the real practice, the search for the self, to begin. The ox depicted in Kuoan's pictures represents the True Self; thus the search is basically a process of discovery of the nature of the self.

The first stage has to do with acknowledging and clarifying the aspiration to realize ourselves. It is that aspiration for clarity that will allow us to deal with the many layers of our conditioning; to bring each one to light, to examine it, to let it go, and to investigate deeper.

In our investigation, we are essentially encountering an idea of a self that is perpetuated through the notion of separateness, a notion that the self is everything that's encapsulated in this bag of skin, distinct from everything else. We are dealing with an idea of a self that we need to assert, protect, and reinforce through our efforts to delineate a boundary between the illusions of what is "inside" and "outside" of the self. We are dealing with an idea of a self that we constantly reaffirm through an internal dialogue.

We talk to ourselves. We are preoccupied with a private conversation that is usually concerned with the past or the future—the past which has already happened and doesn't exist anymore, and the future which hasn't yet happened and similarly doesn't exist. While we talk to ourselves, reifying the self through the incessant chatter of "here I am, this is me, that is them," we miss the moment-to-moment reality of our lives.

When we miss the moment, we miss our life. The moment is where our life takes place. Wrapped up in our inner conversation, most of us go through life only vaguely aware of the moment-to-moment reality. We eat, but we don't taste; we look, but we don't see; we listen, but we don't hear; we love, but we don't feel. We are thinking, preoccupied with our self-perpetuated dramas. All the data of the moment is available to us, but somehow cognition does not take place. Our life slips by and we barely notice it in passing.

Through the stillness and openness of silent sitting in meditation, little by little, an awareness begins to be born. We learn, moment by moment, to be in the moment. We begin to see our internal dialogue. We become aware of how much time we spend chasing thoughts and how little time we spend awake to our lives. In engaging zazen, we notice our thoughts, we let go of our thoughts, and we return our attention to the experience of our breath. We come back to this moment. In letting go of our thoughts, in letting go of the idea of the self, we reclaim our life. We begin to develop the power of concentration, the ability to put our mind where we want it, when we want it there, for as long as we want it there. And that is no small thing. That is the pearl of stillness.

The first stage lasts as long as we need to let go of the baggage we are carrying on our backs. It depends on what we are bringing into the present. There are no shortcuts. We need to deal with all of the thoughts that are churning in our mind, obstructing our clarity. We cannot approach the point of stillness if we have a mind that's like a monkey, jumping all over the place. And yet, we can't simply let go of our thoughts unless we examine them and deal with them. We can ignore, minimize, or deny them for a while, but they're still there. And they will reassert themselves, screaming for attention, steering our actions.

An unexamined life is a perilous life. Real spiritual investigation is not about expression or suppression. It is about investigation and waking up. It is not about sugar-coating our conditioning in spiritual notions and exercises. That's hiding. That's not yet spiritual practice. Practice is exhaustive self-examination. It is in the study of the self that we empower ourselves. In the stillness that emerges we learn to trust ourselves.

The poem describing the first stage of a spiritual journey says:

Vigorously cutting a path through the brambles,
  you search for the ox;

Wide rivers, eternal mountains, the path seems endless.
With strength depleted, and mind exhausted, you cannot
  find it.
There is only the gentle rustle of maple leaves, and the
  cicadas' evening song.

The experience of "strength depleted, mind exhausted" is a familiar one to people who are beginning a spiritual journey. We are searching but we cannot find our way. It seems like there is no end to the struggle. The brambles are the barriers we discover in our lives—the ideas, the postures, the patterns of behavior that obstruct our freedom. They are the cause of our suffering and bring us to practice in the first place. They are encountered directly when we start practicing.

The path is not clear. It is easy to lose track of it. There are numerous choices, forks in the road. Which path is the right path? Do I need a teacher? Can I mix different spiritual practices? That is the undergrowth that we have to struggle our way through. Crossing rivers, entering mountains—the further we go, the more it seems endless. Distractions abound. And that's how we end up very exhausted and depleted. But at the same time the poem tells us that "there is only the gentle rustling of maple leaves, and the cicadas' evening song." The reality that we will come home to one day is right here, right under our noses.

The first stage of practice has to do with learning to let go, with making ourselves empty and receptive. Working with the breath, using the experience of our breath to anchor ourselves in the moment, we become aware of the activity of the mind, its constant running commentary. We begin to quiet and focus the mind, finding the center of our being, returning easily to the still point again and again. When our concentration and the single-pointedness of mind have been developed, we begin to move into the second stage.

Finding Traces of the Ox

Along the river, deep within the forest, you find the traces;

Leaving behind the fragrant grasses, you study the subtle signs.

The tracks, suddenly as clear as the distant sky, lead you into the endless mountains.

There is no place to hide.

In the second stage of the spiritual journey we orient ourselves within the matrix of the teachings provided by the tradition. We note the resonance between the deepest yearnings of our hearts and the direction pointed out by the tradition, the teachers, and the available training, aligning our intent with them.

The poem says:

> Along the river, deep within the forest, you find the traces;
> Leaving behind the fragrant grasses, you study the subtle
>   signs.
> The tracks, suddenly as clear as the distant sky, lead you
>   into the endless mountains.
> There is no place to hide.

As the result of attending to our questions, of letting go of the distractions, concentrating on what is most important to us, we notice the path. When we turn our attention towards it, the path is as clear as daylight. It is nothing other than our lives. The implication of the poem is that what we are seeking is already what we are. It is not something outside of us and our lives. We cannot hide our true nature.

In the second stage a little bit of light begins to shine. We study ourselves; we observe others practicing around us; we read the available literature; and, little by little, spiritual practice starts to make sense. Most importantly we get glimpses of the relationship between spiritual practice and our daily lives. But at this point the appreciation that our life is our practice is intellectual. We understand it. It is not yet visceral. Practice is not yet a whole body-and-mind expression of our life.

During the early phases of the journey, many people are intoxicated by the exotic wrappings of spiritual traditions—the robes, fragrance of incense, sounds of bells, unique gestures, new art forms—the special aura of the sacred. We love to escape into this unusual "other" realm and to disconnect from the mundane dimensions of our lives. We want to jettison what we dislike about ourselves and replace it with the notions and forms that we consider holy and sublime. The novelty and intensity of our new-found spirituality mark a honeymoon period of practice. With time, as the focus of our attention in seated meditation repeatedly settles on our breath and we get familiar with the workings of our mind, the external distractions fade away, spiritual entertainment ends, and the real work begins.

The techniques used at the outset of a spiritual journey tend to sharpen our concentration, broaden our awareness, clarify our intent, and allow us to deepen our trust in ourselves and the process we are engaging. We continue to develop great faith, great doubt, and great determination—the three pillars of sound practice. Some people come into training with an attitude marked by these qualities, while others need to discover and cultivate it. It is through cultivating the questions and trust together with fierce determination that we convert our intellectual understanding into a personal and intimate experience.

During the early forays of exploration into the nature of the self, we get to see the self-imposed limits we have inflicted on our lives and the world around us. We are beginning to practice the illusion of our boundaries, getting familiar with the edges of the unknown. There is movement towards the edge of practice, then a pulling back—a cyclic venture towards the unknown and a retreat back to the safe, but increasingly unsatisfying place of familiar patterns. In engaging our edges, we deepen our confidence.

Because of these brief excursions towards the unknown, the practice has a mysterious air. We tend to be very preoccupied with our practice and *it* can become something separate from everything else. "My practice" may seem to be rarefied, special, subtle, and profound—utterly distinct from washing my face, cooking a meal, or sweeping the floor. This attitude of compartmentalizing our lives, while elevating areas of "sacred" activity, can only serve to create more differentiation than real intimacy.

In the meantime, as we return to the seated meditation of zazen as a regular ingredient of our lives, we continue to develop our power of concentration. In Zen training, we call that capacity to focus our attention on one activity wholeheartedly, *joriki*, the power of concentration. Joriki is essential to genuine and effective spiritual investigation. We can't broaden or deepen our perspective without it.

The power of concentration is not just mental power. It is not just the power to put our mind where we want it to be. It can also manifest itself as a physical capacity. I have seen martial artists who have tapped the power of joriki do extraordinary feats. One young woman who regularly visits our monastery, and who is a practitioner of karate, is able to break two cinder blocks with her elbows. She weighs no more than a hundred pounds, is rather bony, and has an ordinary looking elbow. There are no calluses on it, no bulky muscles. But her concentration is centered and intense. She can leap off the ground into the air and with her foot break two boards being held by someone sitting on the shoulders of someone else—a solid six feet in the air.

The human form is absolutely magnificent when it is fully engaged. Most of us glide through life using only a minuscule fraction of our potential. Joriki taps into our physical, mental, and emotional reserves, and opens our spiritual capacities. One way that our spiritual power begins to manifest is through the emergence of the intuitive aspect of our consciousness. Unfolding and continuous concentration develops our intuition. We become more directly aware of the world. We notice in ways that are not clearly understood but that are very accurate. And this germinating awareness is not mediated by the filters of our ideas and expectations, not dependent on the subject and object polarization of reality. It is immediate and whole. It is the basis of real intimacy, of no separation.

Joriki allows us to cut through the mind's smoke screens and distractions with increasing astuteness. We get to the heart of our questions and dig into them. These questions: What is truth? What is reality? What is life? What is death? can't be dealt with, with a mind that's skipping all over the place. There's no penetrating power in that kind of a mind. Captured repeatedly by the ceaseless stimuli of the world around us, it is scattered, weak, and ineffective.

When the totality of our mind is focused on a single point, its power becomes staggering. Joriki allows us to clearly see the marks of the spiritual path in front of our faces.

Little by little, with increasing concentration and more acute awareness, our thoughts begin to slow down, finally reaching a point where they disappear. The internal dialogue diminishes enough so that for short periods of time, during prolonged and intense stretches of meditation, we have the experience of "body and mind falling away." Falling away of body and mind is the forgetting of the self. When the thoughts disappear, the thinker disappears, because the thought and the thinker are two parts of the same reality; they are interdependent entities. One cannot exist without the other. When that happens, we experience *samadhi*.

Samadhi is the single-pointedness of mind that the Buddha was experiencing when he saw the morning star and realized enlightenment. At the outset, as our concentration settles, periods of samadhi are very brief. But the reverberations of even these brief instances of samadhi immediately spill over into our lives. The experience of forgetting the self is that critical. When in our meditation we have tasted the realm of samadhi, it shows. It shows in the way we walk, the way we listen, the way we talk, the way we move. A change begins to take place, a change in the way we perceive ourselves and the universe.

In most cases, we may not be aware of this shift, but there is good evidence that it has begun to happen. It is most readily confirmed by the changes in our lives—an appearance of new sensibility and attentiveness, and by the way we see and do things and relate with our environment. These shifts are very subtle. They are not dramatic, not a "big deal." Others frequently notice them before we do.

One of the recurrent difficulties that arises at this stage of the journey is the surfacing of many uncertainties. With acknowledgment of the importance of questioning, suddenly everything is under scrutiny. We begin to doubt whether we can even walk. We doubt our most minute amount of understanding of anything. Out of that uncertainty and frustration spring intense emotions. For some people it is plain, raw anger. For other people it is fear or anxiety. Different personalities react differently. In the presence of frustrations some attack, others turn and recoil. Both are valid responses. Both will dissolve as we continue to practice. It is simply a matter of time.

The second stage is about perseverance and patience. Often, people enter spiritual practice with expectations of an immediate breakthrough or earth-shattering insight. Many of us are accustomed to fast-paced, quick-solution, immediate-gratification lifestyles. One of my students had been practicing with a koan in his sitting meditation. He had been studying with me for about three years when he happened to go to California on a job assignment. While there, he decided to do an intensive meditation retreat with my teacher. He began the retreat and went to his first face-to-face interview. He told my teacher that he was studying with me and working on his koan. My teacher asked, "How long have you been working on it?" He said, "Three years." And my teacher immediately rang the bell, ending the interview. He didn't even want to talk to him. Three years? You haven't even started. Go away.

The work of studying the self and getting a glimpse of its real nature can take years. In a sense, it takes a lifetime. People somehow think that they need to accomplish themselves overnight; that if they struggle they are spiritual failures. We need to remember that the struggle is the path. The goal of this endeavor is already present in the moment-to-moment reality of how we conduct our lives. Practice is enlightenment. So, we need to practice; we need to discover; we need to trust ourselves and the process.

Seeing the Ox

The song of the yellow oriole echoes in the forest.

Warm sun, gentle breeze, willows green along the shore.

The ox has no place to turn in the brambles.

THE THIRD STAGE OF THE SPIRITUAL JOURNEY PIVOTS ON getting the first glimpse of the true nature of the self. It is about becoming completely awake and seeing clearly for just a moment.

In the picture corresponding to this stage, we can discern the rump of the ox. Its head is invisible, buried in the grasses and shrubs. The poem says:

> The song of the yellow oriole echoes in the forest.
> Warm sun, gentle breeze, willows green along the shore.
> The ox has no place to turn in the brambles.

It seems like the ox is trying to depart. Attempting to slip away, it ventures into the thicket and gets stuck. Its head and horns are locked in the twisted strands of the undergrowth and it can't escape. Its rump is sticking out, plainly visible, and we see it. We see the ox. We glimpse our True Self.

In getting that first glimpse of the ox, we are not quite clear what it is that we are seeing. We see an animal across the field, in the woods. It seems obvious that it is a white, huge, four-legged beast, but that's about it. It could be a white horse. It could be a white moose. It might not be an ox. Or, it might be an ox. We have a general sense of what we are looking at but we cannot swear that we really saw it. That is the typical breakthrough that most people have in the third stage. Usually this happens in a brief moment of deep samadhi in the midst of stretches of seated meditation. In order for the realization to occur, the six senses have to merge. That is the experience of no-experience—"no eye, ear, nose, tongue, body, and mind." For a very short period of time, the ideas of the self are forgotten, and we see the true nature of reality clearly for the first time.

That moment of directly perceiving reality is *prajna*—wisdom. The line of the poem, "The song of the yellow oriole echoes in the forest. Warm sun, gentle breeze, willows green along the shore" is insight informed by that wisdom. Within the difficulties of our lives, through our practice, we come to a resting point. The True Self becomes conspicuous. What was always there, once hidden, becomes clear as daylight. We dealt with it every day. It passed in front of us but we couldn't see it. We couldn't see it because we never took the time to shine the light of our mind on anything long enough to clearly discern. Our mind was bouncing all over the place—analyzing, judging, comparing, systematizing, filing—humming like an office of heavy-duty computers, constantly processing data with no focus, with no ability to perceive, and no penetrating insight.

Seeing the true nature of the self is the experience of no separation from the totality of the universe. It is usually a fleeting encounter but it is radical in how it touches the texture of our being. Our insight is the unification with all things. It is also unification of intellectual understanding with experience. What we understood intellectually becomes verified experientially. Our practice verifies the truth. The truth is no longer an idea. It is our body and mind. At such a time the truth becomes ours. We become the truth.

Our activities also verify the insights. We begin to actualize our wisdom. The cycle of practice continues ceaselessly: in each stage there is raising the mind of enlightenment; there is practice; there is realizing; and there is actualizing. Seeing is doing. Wisdom begins to manifest as our life. Realization is tangible. It is not philosophical. It is transformative. It is a change of a person's life. If that is not happening, it is usually an indication that we are not fully engaging our practice. And then the spiritual journey remains an abstraction or entertainment.

Running counter to the deepening trust in our experiences is our incredibly insidious tendency to intellectualize. We don't think we've got it unless we can name it. Inevitably, with any amount of insight, we want to be able to talk about it. We want to be able to fit it into our reference system. Of course, absolute wisdom doesn't fit any referential perspectives because it has no limits. It is boundless. But we try anyway, and, in order to make insight fit our data base, we chop off a chunk here, squeeze a few things together there, modify its shape. We push it through the filters of our preconceptions and force it into the container of our knowledge. But what we have now is no longer the experience. It is a static abstraction.

Spring breeze is a definite experience. We can take a jar, run out with it into a warm April morning, and capture some air in it. Put a cap on the jar and label it "spring breeze." What do we have? Obviously, not the spring breeze. It is now an idea, not an ineffable experience. After the first glimpse of the True Self, people quickly latch onto it, make a concept out of it, grasp, and strangle it. That's not it. That misses it.

This attempt to intellectualize our lives is a continuous peril of the spiritual journey. There is no way to avoid it. We do it all the time. We distance ourselves from our lives with our thoughts. We distance ourselves from our clarity with our thoughts. And what rests ahead of us on the spiritual path is the uninterrupted training of letting go of that tendency; of learning how to appreciate and trust the direct experience and the mystery that is unspeakable.

Catching the Ox

Through extraordinary effort you seize the ox.

Still, its will is forceful, and its body spirited.

Sometimes it runs high into the mountains,
    other times it disappears into the mist.

In the fourth stage we begin to get a rudimentary understanding of the nature of the True Self. Yet, despite our increasing ability to appreciate reality directly and accurately, it is still difficult to get our insights to manifest in our lives. It is one thing to see the ox; it is quite another to actually to take hold of it. The poem says:

> *Through extraordinary effort you seize the ox.*
> *Still, its will is forceful, its body spirited.*
> *Sometimes it runs high into the mountains,*
>   *other times it disappears into the mist.*

The first line, "Through extraordinary effort you seize the ox" points to the relationship between our determination and intimacy. Intimacy is real seeing; not the seeing of an object by a subject, but seeing when there is no separation between subject and object. It is the identity of subject and object. Intimacy is seeing with our whole body and mind. It is the breakthrough of perceiving the nature of the True Self. The term *kensho*, frequently used in Zen writings, literally means seeing the nature of the self. But "Still, its will is forceful and its body spirited." That's the ego. We see into the nature of the ego, but it doesn't die easily. It is programmed to reappear, to constantly reassert itself. "Sometimes it runs high into the mountains, other times it disappears into the mist." It becomes very slippery and it is hard to take a definite, experiential hold of it.

With the original breakthrough, wisdom begins to function. Wisdom, in this case, is not the mere amassing of knowledge. It is not the analytical dissection of reality that leads to conventional understanding or explanation. Wisdom is the direct appreciation of the oneness of the universe and the self. But that functioning of wisdom is very inconsistent. It runs hot and cold.

Frequently, our actions are not in accord with our clarity. We know what we should be doing, we know what is right, but that is not what we do. Often, in fact, we do exactly the opposite. An ancient Chinese commentary on this stage says, "He dwelt in the forest a long time, but I caught him today. Infatuation for scenery interferes with his direction. Longing for sweeter grass, he wanders away. His mind is still stubborn and unbridled. If I wish him to submit, I must raise my whip." This is a tremendous and all-pervasive struggle, the stage of the journey when we are beginning to transform the habits developed over a lifetime to accord with our emerging understanding.

At the very same time when we have seen the futility of our ingrained habit patterns, they continue to propagate themselves and spill over into our spiritual activities. Instead of coveting our neighbor's new car, we covet the calligraphy they received from their teacher. Or we begrudge their progress on the spiritual path, seeing them "getting ahead." But coveting is coveting, envy is envy, no matter how we look at it.

After the initial breakthrough, there also appears the tendency to get inflated with our insight—the disease of accomplishment, of objectifying and personalizing our experience. We think that we have acquired something concrete, something substantial that we can point to and feel special about. This is one of the worst possible delusions, one that violates the very foundation of the moral and ethical teachings. To even give rise to the thought that there is a distinction between ordinary beings and Buddhas, a gap between our ordinary mind and our enlightened Buddha mind, is a defilement.

Master Deshan, after his humbling encounter with the old woman selling tea, went to study and train with Master Longtan and, under his careful guidance, realized himself. After his realization experience, he developed an acute case of overblown self-importance. He had come swaggering down from the northern part of China, planning to defeat the southern heretics and show them what the real teachings of Zen were about. The woman selling tea chewed him up and spit him out. He had enough sense to pursue his doubts at that point and entered Longtan's monastery. There he had an enlightenment experience. And his personality immediately reasserted itself. In his haughtiness, and with a dramatic gesture, he burned all of the texts and commentaries on the Diamond Sutra he carried and worshipped. He was still an arrogant fool; a realized fool—he saw the nature of the True Self—but nonetheless a fool.

His arrogant qualities persisted. Next time we encounter him in his journey, he is walking into Master Guishan's monastery, carrying his staff with a bell on the end of it, ringing it in announcement of his arrival. Guishan was a great teacher, accomplished and respected. Deshan took no note of that. He stumbled in, all ego and display, with no intention to greet Guishan. Lost in himself, he walked from east to west in the meditation hall, looked around, and said, "There's nothing, no one." Then he turned and left. When he arrived at the monastery gate, he reconsidered his whole demonstration and said to himself, "Still, I shouldn't be so coarse." He prepared himself to properly meet the teacher with full ceremony.

Meanwhile, from his high seat, Guishan quietly watched all of this with unblinking eyes. Deshan approached Guishan's seat, spread his bowing mat, prostrated himself, and exclaimed, "Teacher!" As Guishan was reaching for his fly-whisk, a symbol of his teacher status, Deshan shouted, got up and departed for good. Guishan, turning to the head monk standing nearby, said, "Someday that lad will go to the summit of a solitary peak, build himself a grass hut, and go on scolding the Buddhas and reviling the Ancestors." Someday. Guishan wasn't quite approving Deshan. He poured some water on him and cooled him off a bit.

Despite insight, despite realization of the nature of reality, conditioning is still present. We have a breakthrough. For a moment there's clarity, for a moment the light of our mind shines. Then, very quickly, it clouds over, because our conditioning is fathomless. It's been going on for a lifetime, supported everywhere. It doesn't disappear overnight. From this point on, our spiritual journey is about letting go of our conditioning in view of our clarity; it is about actualization of our insight. This process continues forever. Realization followed by actualization, insight becoming action.

STAGE FIVE

Taming the Ox

The whip and tether cannot be put aside or the ox
may wander into mud-filled swamps.

When patiently trained to trust, it becomes gentle
and can be unfettered.

Then, freely, it follows your way.

Our training has advanced to where we have verified for ourselves the natural order of reality. We are pretty clear about how our mind works; how our habit patterns affect our lives; what the trigger points are that bring up our anger, greed, or fear; how we fit into the universal scheme of things. We begin to discern clearly but we still remain relatively powerless in uprooting our conditioned responses. They still arise. Even though we know why we are getting irritated with people, we still respond with anger or fear, and act on them blindly. The process of taming our ego is a persistent turning of our theoretical knowledge into a vivid and relevant expression. This stage is characterized by a repeated movement from realization to actualization, the manifestation of our developing clarity as our life. We use everyday circumstances to discover where our buttons are and how we slip into the reactive and habitual modes of being. We use our practice of awareness to open up the possibility of living more harmoniously. The whole practice is gradually beginning to come together and is less of a struggle. But there is still the nose-ring, the need for the discipline to actualize what is realized.

The poem says,

> *The whip and tether cannot be put aside or the ox may*
> *   wander into mud-filled swamps.*
> *When patiently trained to trust, it becomes gentle and can*
> *   be unfettered.*
> *Then, freely, it follows your way.*

There is impeccable diligence at this stage of the journey. We need to be totally honest in our practice. We need to keep examining ourselves. The ego is very persistent in reestablishing itself. It slips through the gaps of our attention and recreates itself in new and subtle ways. Spiritual justifications for our misguided actions abound. "The whip and tether cannot be put aside, or the ox may wander into mud-filled swamps." And to extract ourselves from the mud-filled spiritual swamps is especially difficult.

"When patiently trained to trust, it becomes gentle and can be unfettered." With all that accumulated effort and experience behind us, there are times now when we can release the ox. "Then, freely it follows your way." We begin to be able to trust ourselves completely. Within the discipline and diligence arises the ability to relax and be guided by our intuition. We learn to live what we have seen and realized, and to do so effortlessly and spontaneously.

After the initial breakthrough, the spiritual practice has to do with dismantling our habitual patterns and conditioning. That is tougher than any of us can imagine. The illusion of the self is wrapped up in hundreds of threads of thought, activity, and posture—*our* ways of doing things—our way of dealing with people, our way of working, our way of eating, our way of driving a car, playing with children, interacting with animals, appreciating the wilderness. All of these dimensions of life are inundated with our habit patterns, patterns that are dualistic and associated with our conditioning.

The process of undoing these patterns, taming the ox, is very gradual. There are no grand experiences of clarity here, no world-shattering discernments. It's day by day meticulous work. We need to get used to and friendly with the spiritual plateau. It seems like there is no progress on this plateau. It feels like we are treading water. Because there are no quantum leaps, it seems like nothing is happening. We are just kind of sitting there. So we need to learn to love the plateau and understand that the plateau is just as important as the steep slopes that we climb during this journey.

"When patiently trained it becomes gentle and can be unfettered. Then, it freely follows your way." With practice and the growing trust, working samadhi begins to develop. The samadhi is no longer just the concentration that's taking place when we sit in zazen. It begins to manifest in activity now. We're able to stay with what we are doing and not disconnect from the moment by chasing thoughts, preoccupied with something other than the activity at hand, wishing we weren't there. That single-mindedness on any and all facets of life is working samadhi. It functions when we're listening and when we're working; it functions when we're doing whatever we're doing. And it is not some kind of zombie trance. It's our aliveness and presence, moment to moment to moment. Each instant is lucid and complete.

Within that working samadhi, *karuna*—real compassion—begins to appear. Compassion is wisdom in action. It is not merely doing good. At the beginning of practice, many of us experience an overwhelming, bleeding-heart impetus to save the world, mixed with equally overwhelming despair that there are just too many problems and too few resources. As practice matures, our awkward attempts or pessimistic withdrawals are replaced by genuine compassion arising from practice and realization. We see what we can do and we do it. We do it without even reflecting or knowing that we're doing it. Compassion happens. It happens the way we grow our hair. It is that simple and that mysterious.

It is towards the end of the fifth stage that we are able to relax a little bit in our practice. The main peril here is that if we let go of our diligence too much, we can fall back into the old ruts of conditioning. That can happen very easily, especially if our practice is not consistent. That's why it is critical to maintain our regular daily meditation. Grounding ourselves in zazen, we repeatedly re-establish the still point, the clean slate from which we can encounter ourselves and the world afresh. If we stop sitting it's easy to backslide and get right back into our habit patterns. And now we have at our disposal a wealth of spiritual jargon to explain our actions. We can end up stuck in an endless cycle of constricting justifications that sound very convincing, rather than letting go of the cages we constructed. Without zazen, we can shape our practice to fit our egocentric notions and preferences. Such a self-styled spiritual path is one of the most sticky and difficult places to extricate ourselves from. The challenge confronting us is the fine tuning of our effort. We need to keep our practice alive and vital.

The movement from realization to actualization applies at every stage in training after the original breakthrough. At every step along the way, every year of my practice, I would say to myself, "This is it. I've got it." And then, two weeks later, "Now this is really it. Now I've got it." And on and on and on, continual revelations. Everything becomes clearer and clearer. And how clear is clear? It's endless. It continues. There are no edges to it.

STAGE SIX

Riding the Ox Home

Following the winding road you ride the ox home.

The sound of your rustic flute pervades the evening
haze.

Each note, each song: feeling unbounded.

Beyond lips and mouth.

At this phase of the spiritual journey we start to navigate the complexities of our life with ease. The poem focuses on this effortless activity that emerges in our daily encounters:

Following the winding road you ride the ox home.
The sound of your rustic flute pervades the evening haze.
Each note, each song: feeling unbounded.
Beyond lips and mouth.

"Following the winding road, you ride the ox home" describes a state of relaxation amidst difficulties. The path is full of turns and intersections, hills and valleys, but we are travelling with ease. "Beyond lips and mouth" means beyond words and ideas. It is an image of the whole body-and-mind directly experiencing the moment—an effortless activity, involvement without affectations.

A sense of unity with the myriad of phenomena and events in our life begins to appear. Working samadhi is functioning smoothly. "Each note, each song, feeling unbounded" points to the appreciation of the all-encompassing nature of each thing, each particle, each moment.

We have reached a stage of no return. There's no turning back. Up till now, we tended to waver in our commitment. Our determination ran hot and cold. The strength of our spiritual intent largely depended on our individual personality and predispositions: our desires, needs, motives, and effort. Once we get this far in seeing the nature of the self clearly, it's hard to turn back. Almost impossible. It's like being caught in a vortex of reality and sanity. We just go on and on, without any definitive sense of how it is happening. We trust ourself, the process, life, and the whole catastrophe. We are returning home to the natural order of things.

An ancient commentary on this stage says, "The struggle is over. Gain and loss are assimilated. I sing the song of the village woodsman, and play the tunes of the children. Astride the ox, I observe the clouds above. Onward I go, no matter who may wish to call me back."

In Buddhist lore, an image of the plum tree represents Shakyamuni Buddha, an enlightened person, or an accomplished spiritual teacher. At this juncture of our practice, the plum has appeared on the tree. The fruit of our practice is still slightly bitter. It's not yet fully mature and ripe. No one would want to eat it but, nonetheless, it's a plum. For complete maturation to occur, we still have to experience what is called the Great Death, a complete obliteration of any remaining notions of a self-entity that is separate and distinct from others.

The three poisons—greed, anger, and ignorance—are increasingly beginning to manifest as the three virtues of compassion, wisdom, and enlightenment. That transformation confirms our intimacy with the absolute nature of reality. What we experientially understand and what we do are closer in harmony.

Where in the previous stages, the experience of "falling away of body and mind" presented us with some appreciation of how emptiness is the fundamental condition underlying all differentiation, we now start to see how emptiness relates to forms. In the third and fourth stages we caught a glimpse of the absolute. Some clarification occurred in the next stage. Now, we emerge out of that experience of emptiness and begin to see the relationship of form and emptiness, and how the absolute basis of reality informs our everyday activities.

A common complication of this stage is referred to as creating reality patterns. We try to figure the whole thing out. We package what was directly experienced into dogma. And, as before, when we intellectualize our experiences, when we try to grasp reality, make it rigid and file it away, it becomes an abstraction of what was once tangible and loses its capacity to enliven and nourish the situation. We slip into the compulsion of creating patterns, unable to rest completely and ceaselessly in the suchness of the moment.

Everything that we encounter in Zen training, all of the devices and skillful measures, are provisional means to get us to see the truth. All of it—every form and ritual, the words, ideas, koans, insights—is specifically designed to ultimately self-destruct. We really can't hold on to anything because there is nothing to hold on to. During our spiritual training we are presented with different practices and techniques, appropriate ways to see the True Self. We take them up, chew them, fully digest them, make them our own, and let them go. And continue on. When we get to the peak of the mountain—the clarity, boundlessness, and compassion of enlightenment—we chew it up, fully digest it, let it go, and keep going. Endlessly.

Forgetting the Ox

Astride the ox, you reach home.

Now at rest, the ox is forgotten.

With the bright sun high in the sky, you are in blissful repose.

Whip and tether are abandoned behind the thatched hut.

The seventh stage of the journey is called reaching home. The ox is transcended. The poem says:

Astride the ox, you reach home.
Now at rest, the ox is forgotten.
With the bright sun high in the sky, you are in blissful
  repose.
Whip and tether are abandoned behind the thatched hut.

The struggle has ended. A sense of peacefulness and relaxation pervades. The world is illuminated and a feeling of bliss permeates it.

The ox is gone, but the person remains. An ancient Chinese comment on this stage is, "All is one, not two. We only make the ox a temporary subject. It is as the relationship of a rabbit in a trap, a fish in a net, as gold in dross or the moon emerging from a cloud. One path of clear light travels throughout endless time."

This is what Master Linji referred to as "the True Person of no

Rank." Commenting on the True Person, he said, "Within this lump of red flesh there is a True Person of no Rank that goes in and out of the senses. Each of you, if you have not seen it yet—Look! Look!"

When the ego gets out of the way and the self is thoroughly forgotten, compassion manifests itself easily and readily. The training is now effortless. I try to reassure people that practice doesn't continue being a chore for the rest of our lives. I would have never persisted if I needed to force myself to do it, or if it were a continuously painful or unhappy undertaking to sit in meditation or do long silent retreats. It definitely gets easier and easier with time, and the struggle eventually ends. Practice becomes a joyful experience. We actually look forward to it.

In the beginning stages of training we are engaging our lives in ways that we never did before. We are examining ourselves honestly and exhaustively. We are approaching all of life with a student's mind. Most of us spend a lifetime hiding from ourselves. Pursuing a genuine spiritual practice demands that we study the self without flinching or turning our gaze away—a very difficult proposition. But at this point it all happens with ease.

There's no abiding place now, no place to locate ourselves, no nesting spot. Nothing is fixed, nothing lacking, and nothing extra.

We are not clinging to anything. Trusting ourselves and our life completely, we don't need to grasp onto anything.

That freedom from grasping and holding on doesn't mean that we don't have or use things. It's just that we don't attach to them. There's a critical difference between those two paradigms. Not to attach is to truly care, to move freely within any circumstances and conditions. When we see the transitory nature of things, we see that nothing is fixed and there can be no holding on. That is the perfection of "nothing lacking and nothing extra."

When we are capable of letting go with ease, when we don't grab at things or cling to them, there is the lurking danger of dismissing the importance and usefulness of practice and discipline. We allow life to happen without trying to direct or choreograph it. We trust the process implicitly without need for props and control. The pitfall is that we may forget the value of the training forms in helping others.

It's very attractive at this point to want to renounce the messiness of the world and disconnect from the rigidity of the forms. We just want to go off and be a hermit. Why do we need robes? Why do we need liturgy? Indeed, why practice? Just because the forms self-destructed for us at this point, we shouldn't forget their general value and necessity. They will help, nourish, and heal others. They helped, nourished, and healed us. The form works. We need to continue to appreciate that and not be self-centered in the way we understand the usefulness of the skillful means and power of the tradition.

Looking at our appreciation of the relationship between the absolute and relative, in the seventh stage, wisdom and compassion begin to mutually arise and compassion begins to function freely in our lives. What evolved and deepened in the course of training up until this point is our ability to see the absolute basis of reality, to clarify that perspective, and to see how that absolute basis really functions in the world of phenomena. The next step needs to be the interpretation of absolute and relative, the complete merging of all dualities.

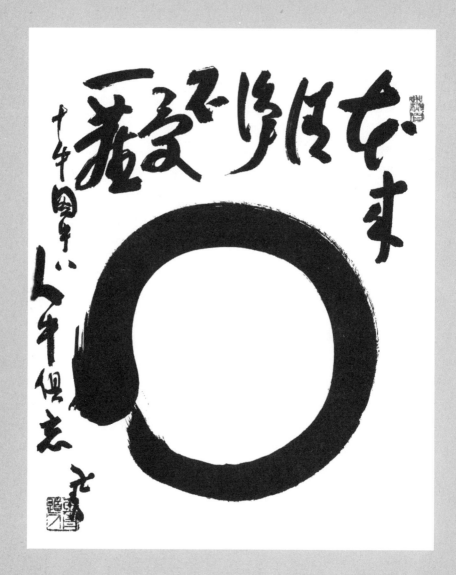

Transcending the Ox

Whip, tether, self, and ox all have merged,
   no traces remain.

The vast blue sky cannot be reached by thoughts;
   how can a snowflake abide in a raging fire?

Having reached home, you are in accord with the
   ancient way.

THE EIGHTH STAGE IS MARKED BY THE COMPLETE FALLING away of body and mind. The ox and the person are gone. Self and other are forgotten. The poem says:

> Whip, tether, self, and ox all have merged,
>   no traces remain.
> The vast blue sky cannot be reached by thoughts;
>   how can a snowflake abide in a raging fire?
> Having reached home, you are in accord with the
>   ancient way.

That "vast blue sky that cannot be reached by thoughts" is the experience of "no eye, ear, nose, tongue, body, mind." This is the full realization of emptiness; not the mere glimpse of the third stage, but a complete and thorough falling away of body and mind, self and other. The absolute body fills the universe. At this point, mountains are not mountains, rivers are not rivers. The mind is void of any constraints. There is no searching for a state of enlightenment. There is no persisting in delusions. Our lives don't fall into either of these extremes.

There are three bodies of the Buddha, an enlightened being— *dharmakaya, sambhogakaya,* and *nirmanakaya.* These three bodies are the last three stages of the ox-herding series. Dharmakaya, the absolute basis of reality and negation of all things, is the eighth stage. Sambhogakaya, the body of bliss or the reward body, is the ninth stage. And nirmanakaya, "the bliss bestowing hands," the physical body and the teachings of the Buddha, is the tenth and final stage.

An associated comment on the eighth stage is, "Mediocrity is gone. Mind is clear of limitation. I seek no state of enlightenment, neither do I remain where no enlightenment exists. Since I linger in neither condition, eyes cannot see me. If hundreds of birds strew my path with flowers, such praise would be meaningless."

One of the diseases of this stage is what we call in Zen the "dead person breathing," the resting place of absolute wisdom that feels no pain. It is possible to hide here, using our accomplishments as an escape. Half of the cases in the classic koan collections address this tendency to detach and dwell aloof in the aftermath of realization. Teachers warn about the danger of getting to this place and dropping out, living our life in solitude, not being aware of the world and its needs. In some schools of Buddhism, this is the highest level of spiritual development. A person completes their journey when they have attained *shunyata*, the all-pervading emptiness. They've reached the height of spiritual development; it's very personal and it has nothing to do with the rest of the world. There isn't any rest of the world. Everything is cut off. Everything has dropped away.

It is of critical importance to have the support of an accomplished teacher at this juncture. It is very easy to validate ourselves upon realization, derailing the whole process of training. The teacher will keep the student engaged, not allowing them to confuse the experience of the absolute with the complete, functioning realization and actualization. To realize the absolute is not yet enlightenment. It is the peak, yet it's very important to continue the journey down the other side of the mountain, back into the business and the complications of the world so that our realization is tested and actualized in everything that we do. That is perpetually challenging and difficult. And that's why it is important to be guided by a spiritual teacher.

Returning to the Source

Having returned to the source, effort is over.

The intimate self sees nothing outside, hears nothing outside.

Still, the endless river flows tranquilly on, the flowers are red.

THE NINTH STAGE IS THE REACHING OF THE ORIGINAL source.

> *Having returned to the source, effort is over.*
> *The intimate self sees nothing outside, hears nothing*
>   *outside.*
> *Still, the endless river flows tranquilly on, the flowers*
>   *are red.*

"Having returned to the source the effort is over." Basically, life is uncomplicated. It is not all complexity and struggle. Once we are at this stage, it is not what we thought it was. From the deluded perspective of our mind, life is infinitely confusing and problematic. It is painful and filled with suffering. But when we have traced the light of our mind back to its source, it becomes clear that life is very simple and natural.

"The intimate self sees nothing outside, hears nothing outside."

The reason for that is that everything is inside. We have swallowed the whole universe! Yet, in spite of that, "The endless river flows tranquilly on, and the flowers are red." Just like that! Thusness. This very moment itself. And now, again, mountains are mountains.

A commentary elaborates, "From the beginning the truth is clear. Poised in silence, I observe the forms of integration and disintegration. One who is not attached to form, need not be re-formed. The water is emerald. The mountain is indigo, and I see that which is creating, and that which is destroying." To return to the source is to realize that things were perfect from the start. Realization is really nothing special.

The ninth stage is sambhogakaya, the reward body of the Buddha. Sambhogakaya is essentially the state of enjoying the truth that one has embodied. The reward body is an incentive as we want all sentient beings to experience that clarity. It is also in the ninth stage that integration and disintegration are clearly present. The impermanence and the interdependence are constantly around us. We see it in nature and among people.

Our activity of compassion is now the manifestation of our life without us being aware of it. When we are realized, our activities accord with circumstances. We are able to respond with ease and precision to whatever comes up.

We see how wisdom and compassion inform the most difficult circumstances of our everyday life; how they are obstructed by the infinity of things in the world of differentiation.

We have begun the process of descending the mountain, coming back into the marketplace—the space and time of relationships, work, and endless challenges. Responding according to circumstances means being able to respond to the imperative, seeing clearly in every situation that which is destroying and that which is creating. We discern what needs to be done and how to do it; sometimes knowing how not to do it—how to stay out of the way and allow things to take care of themselves. This is where doing good has fully transformed into compassion. Activity becomes a spontaneous and attuned way of responding. At times, our actions may not appear like doing good, but they are appropriate and compassionate.

From the perspective of a teacher-student relationship, there is a merging of the teacher and the student. They are indistinguishable in their way of seeing and acting, although they still maintain their individuality. I realize the same truth as my teacher but I am not the same as my teacher. So it is with my successors. They are not my clones. The student "descends the mountain," and comes back to the marketplace to teach, formally or informally, in their own way. They are committed to helping all beings on their journey to realization and freedom. The transmission of the moral and ethical teachings and the lineage—an aspect of the formal mind-to-mind transmission between teacher and student in the Zen tradition—is completed at this stage.

Entering the Marketplace

Entering the marketplace barefoot and
unadorned.

Blissfully smiling, though covered with dust
and ragged of clothes.

Using no supernatural power, you bring the
withered trees spontaneously into bloom.

ARRIVING AT THE TENTH STAGE, YOU ENTER THE MARKET-place. This is nirmanakaya, the physical body and the teachings of the Buddha manifesting in the world for the benefit of others.

In the ox-herding pictures, the youngster who started out on this search returns to the world as an old sage. By the time the journey is over the child has disappeared. Obviously, a lengthy period of time has passed. Although the moment of realization is just that, a moment, the process of studying the self and clarifying the nature of reality doesn't happen overnight. It doesn't even end with the old sage. It continues endlessly. The spiritual path of Zen is a ceaseless practice.

Completing formal training doesn't mean we are not aware of ourselves anymore, or that we stop working on ourselves. It just means that a fundamental change in how we appreciate the self and reality has occurred, and we are able to actualize that view in our lives. Still, zazen continues. It permeates everything. The danger of the unexamined life persists. There is always more to be learned and applied. The limits of the knowable are unknowable.

Entering the marketplace barefoot and unadorned.
Blissfully smiling, though covered with dust and ragged of
   clothes.
Using no supernatural power, you bring the withered trees
   spontaneously into bloom.

"Entering the marketplace barefoot and unadorned" is an image of ordinariness. This relaxation and comfort are not about disregarding the circumstances. It is not about being stupid. It is about perfect harmony. If we walked into the marketplace—the bank office or the hospital—barefoot, we would definitely stand out. Entering into the market place is about being invisible. We are not identifiable as anything other than an ordinary person because that is exactly who we are. That is what has been realized.

"Blissfully smiling, though covered with dust and ragged of clothes" indicates that we possess nothing. Having nothing, we are not holding on to anything. There is no more clinging. Objects have lost their power to seduce us with their importance. They are useful, but it is not necessary to covet them, grab them, accumulate them, or attach to them for the sake of our security or well-being. If they arrive, they arrive; if they need to go, they go.

When I first met my teacher, Maezumi Roshi, I was very grateful for his appearance in my life. I wanted to express my appreciation so I gave him a very special photograph I had taken. It was the last copy of an image that was excruciatingly difficult to print. Originally, I made five or six images before the negative was damaged. I had sold all but this one print at exhibitions. And I loved that picture. I wanted to keep it for myself. But I was so taken by my first meeting with Roshi that I presented it to him as a gift. It was a gift of my heart. It was the most precious thing I could offer him, and that's why I gave it to him. Three months later, when I started to formally study with him, I visited the house of one of his students living in the area. There, on the wall of one of the hallways, was my picture! I got really upset. I couldn't understand. I gave him my heart and he just handed it to somebody else! I asked the student, "Where'd you get that?" He said, "Oh, I was admiring it at Roshi's house and he gave it to me."

Two years later I got a clearer picture of my teacher's attitude about nonattachment. I happened to walk into his house one morning, a few days after a famous sculptor had chiseled an incredibly gorgeous head of Maitreya Buddha for Roshi. It was big, with Western features, which was very rare at that time. It sat like a jewel on the mantelpiece. As I walked into the living room it socked me right in the forehead and I exclaimed, "Wow! Roshi, what a beautiful piece! Where'd you get it?" "Oh, so-and-so gave it to me." "It's amazing!" "Here, take it!" he said. As he handed me the statue, I looked beyond him and saw his wife standing in the kitchen doorway, her eyeballs almost falling out of her head. The woman was an artist, and I knew that she knew the real value of that sculpture. I knew I shouldn't take it. So I said, "No, no, no, no, Roshi." And he said "Oh, yes, yes, yes." "No, no, no." "Yes, yes, yes." "No, no, no." "Yes, yes, yes." Finally, I insisted forcefully, and put the head back on the mantel. Roshi's wife relaxed. But that's the way he was. He was like that with everything. No exceptions. Although he had things around him, he did not hold on. He didn't cling to anything.

"Using no supernatural power, you bring the withered trees spontaneously to bloom." We have the ability to give boundlessly, to nourish, and to heal. We can even manifest that simply by being present. We continuously communicate our being with every action, posture, word, and thought. One person can walk into a crowded room and suddenly the place will fill with static and tension. Another person enters and there is a feeling of peace and calm. We create an atmosphere. Someone who is developed spiritually creates a very nourishing aura that attracts and soothes people. The Dalai Lama has that feeling around him. It is even palpable when you watch him on film. His way of being is that pure and uncomplicated.

The spiritual ripeness of the tenth stage is uncontrived, unpretentious, and organic. The plum that has grown to maturity in the ninth stage has now fallen off the tree of its own accord. The tree let go of the plum; the plum let go of the tree. It's mutual. The plum falls, and where it lands seeds take root and new plum trees are formed. This process continues, generation after generation.

At this point, the formality has totally disappeared from the teacher-student relationship. At times, there is a reversal of the roles—the teacher becomes the student, the student becomes the teacher. The merging has become complete. They are no longer two separate entities. In a sense, the teacher disappears. There's no longer a teacher, and everything teaches. Formal training is over. Transmission or Dharma sanction is the final step in formal training, and the student is now totally on their own. They can manifest their life in many different ways, which does not mean necessarily appearing formally as a Zen teacher. The student may reenter the world and just disappear, or may become a parish priest, or may live a hermit's life on the mountainside. But the fact is, their teaching will be manifesting in all circumstances, all the time. It may not happen in the way I have chosen to do it, in a monastery setting with robes and bells; it's up to the new teacher. But even if the teaching is not immediately visible, it is also not possible to hide it or to hold it back.

Coming down off the mountain into the marketplace, we're in the marketplace but have not left the mountain. No trace of enlightenment remains. Master Dogen talked about this traceless enlightenment in a passage quoted partially in the introduction: "To study the Buddha way is to study the self. To study the self is to forget the self. To forget the self is to be enlightened by the ten thousand things. To be enlightened by the ten thousand things is to cast off body and mind of self and other. No trace of enlightenment remains, and this traceless enlightenment continues endlessly."

The essential and defining quality of the tenth stage is present in the first stage—the beginner's mind. The end and the beginning are about the innocent mind, the naivete, the openness, the receptiveness of a real student. This trait is developed fully in the process of coming down off the mountain's lofty peak, where no traces of our realization remain.

There is no sense of doing. The wind blows from the west, and all the leaves gather in the east. Master Deshan, after his encounter with the woman tea-seller and after years of study with Master Longtan, eventually became one of the great teachers in T'ang

Dynasty China, maybe one of the greatest in the Golden Age of Zen. He was known among the practitioners throughout the country for his rigorous standards of training and unwavering demand for clarity among his disciples. He frequently used the stick to urge his students on. He would ask a question. If a student could answer, they got thirty blows of the stick. If they couldn't answer, they got thirty blows of the stick. If they both answered and didn't answer: thirty blows of the stick. If they neither answered nor didn't answer: thirty blows of the stick! There was no way to escape him. He was like a tiger and students were terrified of him.

One day, toward the end of his life, he came wandering down the stairs from his room, carrying his bowls for a ceremonial community meal. Xuefeng, who was the cook at the time, intervened, "Oh master, where are you going with your bowls? The drum hasn't sounded, the bell hasn't rung, it's not time for lunch." And this fierce teacher just looked at him, said, "Oh," and went back to his room.

Xuefeng, happily stunned, figured that he defeated his mentor in that exchange, so he started bragging. The word got around the monastery and reached the head monk Yantou, who decided to check on Xuefeng. Xuefeng told him the story, clearly thinking that his assertiveness sent Deshan scurrying. Hearing all this, Yantou said, "Well, great master that he is, old Deshan still hasn't realized the last word of Zen." Yantou's opinion about his teacher spread through the community like wildfire. Everybody was buzzing about it: "The Old Man doesn't know the last word of Zen! The head monk said so!" Finally, Deshan heard of Yantou's comment and summoned him. He asked, "What's wrong? Don't you approve of me?" Yantou leaned over and whispered something to him. This seemed to satisfy Deshan.

The next day Deshan came down to give his daily talk in the main hall. He mounted the rostrum and delivered a discourse totally unlike anything he had ever presented in all his years of teaching. When he finished the talk, Yantou jumped up out of his seat into the middle of the hall, clapped his hands, and laughing, said, "At last, at last! The Old Man has realized the last word of Zen! No one can ever make light of him again!"

In this account, Deshan is a diametrically different person from the arrogant young seeker he was at the beginning of his spiritual journey. He displays no trace of enlightenment. There is no stink of holiness or arrogance about him. This is Deshan who bends with the wind; Deshan with no agenda. Unequivocally, he is not a great enlightened master, but an old, ordinary person living in a monastery. He is an embodiment of complete integration of absolute and relative. The two are indistinguishable now. They work completely in accord with one another.

The peril at this stage of the journey is that in acknowledging our inherent perfection we forget the critical value of the skillful means. We throw out the baby with the bathwater. All of the devices and forms simply help us realize what is inherently there. All of them are specifically designed to disintegrate when their usefulness is exhausted. And, at this point of our training, having seen through all of the forms, we realize that they are provisional. In reality, there isn't a thing anybody can give anybody else. Everybody needs to accomplish themselves. Every person has everything they need. They are fully equipped Buddhas. They are born Buddhas and will die Buddhas. The only way to transform our life is to realize it personally. And the path of realization of our inherent perfection is covered with provisional, skillful means.

Master Bankei was an enlightened teacher in Japan. He realized himself when he was quite young. When he started to teach, he went around, saying to people, "You don't have to do anything. You don't have to meditate. Buddhism is not necessary! Just live in the Unborn!" All of his talks were essentially the message of "Just live in the Unborn." Well, nobody realized it! He wasn't very successful.

It is true—all we have to do is to realize the Unborn—but how?

The "how" is the form of skillful means. Form is indispensable. There are people who have spontaneously realized themselves; no question about it. But they are the exceptions, the spiritual geniuses who come one in a million. Ceaseless practice assures our realization no matter what our qualifications and credentials; no matter what our karma.

Zen is an incredible practice, a profound and subtle teaching. It is very likely one of the most highly evolved and refined spiritual practices to appear in human history. It has been going on for 2,500 years and some of the finest minds all over the world have refined it. We're very fortunate to have an opportunity to encounter and engage Zen training. As recently as forty years ago that opportunity didn't exist for Westerners. When I first began struggling with my questions about human consciousness and spirituality, there were no books on Zen. Now there's a glut of them. There were no genuine teachers, either. You could always go to Asia, but there was no guarantee that you were going to find anybody authentic or that you would be admitted into a monastery. To find Zen teachings and practice in our own country, manifesting in our own language, and in forms that are familiar to us, is a very rare and important occasion. It was brought here at no small cost and with an incredible amount of courage by the Asian masters that preceded the current new generations of American teachers. It took an equally monumental amount of ingenuity and perseverance to make the teachings accessible and relevant in this new land. Americans, after all, are difficult students.

But it happened. The Dharma is now in our hands—your hands and my hands. What we do with it is entirely up to each one of us. But we should always keep in mind that we are involved in more than just a personal clarification of our own lives and the experience of enlightenment. We *are* the appearance of Zen in the West. The full implications of that are yet to be seen.

Historian Arnold Toynbee said that hundreds of years from now, when people look back to this period of time, the turn of the millennium, the most important event affecting the subsequent centuries is not going to be the discovery of atomic energy or space travel or computers or any of the remarkable leaps and achievements of our technological civilization. It will be an incident that most people are hardly aware of: the coming of Buddhism from East to West.

Each and every Zen practitioner, each and every one of us, is a part of that process. The teachings are available to us. What we do in our practice creates a precedent, one that's very demanding and that will challenge us constantly. We must not water down the teachings. We must sustain them in an authentic manner. We must practice them with sincerity, the same way they were engaged in T'ang-dynasty China or in Kamakura Japan when Zen first landed on those shores. That's no small thing to ask of ourselves. It's a big deal. But realizing ourselves and transforming our lives is also a big deal: the most important thing we could do. When we practice in our solitude we practice for all sentient beings. And when we realize ourselves, we verify the enlightenment of our ancestors—the past— and we verify the enlightenment of our successors—the future. So please really put yourself into this practice and take care of this Great Matter.

May your journey be fruitful and may your life go well.

Glossary

DHARMAKAYA   One of the three kayas, bodies of the Buddha; the body of the great order, essential reality; the unity of the Buddha with the existing universe.

JORIKI   Power of concentration developed through the practice of meditation that allows a person to place their focus of attention where they choose for extended periods of time.

KARMA   The universal law of cause and effect, linking action's underlying intention to that action's consequences; it equates the actions of body, speech, and thought as potential sources of consequences.

KARUNA   Compassion, active sympathy, based on the enlightened experience of oneness of all beings; activity of prajna, wisdom.

KENSHO   "Seeing into one's own nature"; first experience of realization.

KOAN   An apparently paradoxical statement or question used in Zen training to induce in students an intense level of doubt, allowing them to cut through conventional and conditioned descriptions of reality and see directly into their true nature.

NIRMANAKAYA   One of the three bodies of the Buddha; the earthly body and manifestation that a Buddha assumes to guide all sentient beings toward liberation.

PRAJNA   Wisdom; not that which is possessed but that which is directly and thoroughly experienced.

SAMADHI   State in which the mind is absorbed in concentration, free from distractions; the essential nature of the self can be experienced within samadhi.

SAMBHOGAKAYA   One of the three bodies of Buddha; "body of bliss," or reward body.

SHAKYAMUNI BUDDHA   Siddhartha Gautama, the historical Buddha and the founder of Buddhism; he was a prince of the Shakya clan, living in northern India in the sixth century B.C..

SHUNYATA   Void; central principle of Buddhism that recognizes the emptiness of all composite entities, without reifying nothingness; resolution of all dualities.

ZAZEN   Sitting meditation, taught in Zen as the most direct way to enlightenment; the practice of the realization of one's own true nature.